1·50

CASTLES OF BRITAIN

Castles of Britain

A Balfour Book, printed and published by Photo Precision Ltd.,
St. Ives, Huntingdon, England

FIRST EDITION 1973

PRINTED AND PUBLISHED IN GREAT BRITAIN BY
BALFOUR PUBLICATIONS (PHOTO PRECISION LTD)
ST IVES, HUNTINGDON

ISBN 0 85944 002 8

Foreword

Our castles reflect centuries of social and political history. What is the story of Girnigoe, or Hurstmonceux or Carreg Cennen? Who built them? When were they built? Why were they built? What happened to them? To these and to countless other questions the answers are sometimes known precisely and in other cases they remain little more than the subjects of conjecture or uncertainty even among the experts.

Seventy-six castles are briefly described and illustrated in this publication. Twenty-eight of them are English, twenty-four of them are Scottish and twenty-four of them are Welsh. Although very many more have had to be omitted, those selected are thought to represent an interesting cross-section through the vast choice available. Almost without exception they are situated in delightful surroundings which make visits to them all the more enjoyable. Where it was thought to be necessary, the index includes an indication as to how the castles can best be approached by road.

This publication does not pretend to be a book for the expert. It is intended in the first place to stimulate a wider general interest in castles and then, perhaps, to encourage people to delve more deeply into the wealth of literature that is available to devotees of the history of a subject that has so many fascinating facets.

Although castles comprise such a valuable part of our heritage, the need to preserve them for posterity has been belatedly recognized. Neglect and even wanton destruction were all too common in former times and it is really only during the course of the present century that co-ordinated efforts have been made to maintain and to improve their condition. The Department of the Environment, the National Trust, the National Trust for Scotland and many of the private owners, working in concert, are today doing wonderful work that is much more fully appreciated by the public at large than ever was the case before. Television, radio and colour photography have also done much to widen the extent of public interest in this very rewarding subject.

English Castles

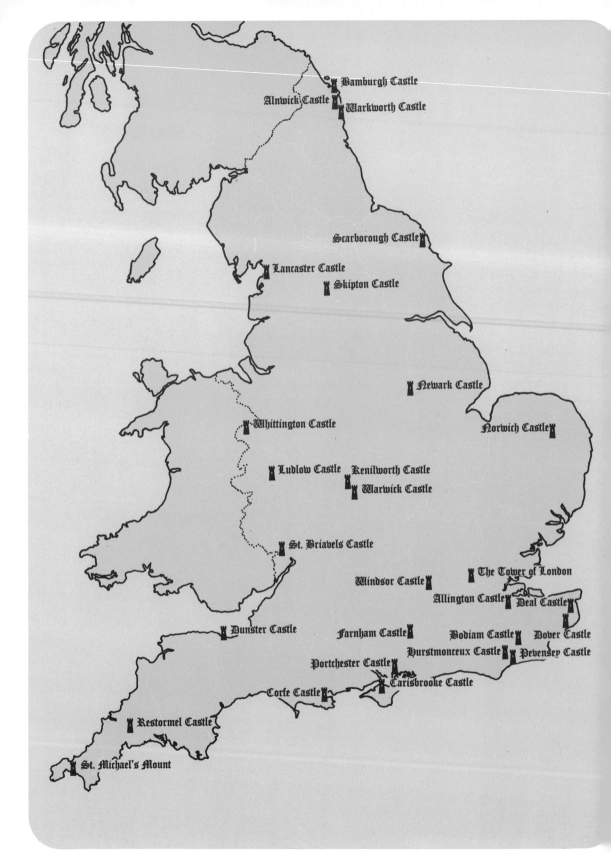

Bamburgh Castle
Alnwick Castle
Warkworth Castle
Scarborough Castle
Lancaster Castle
Skipton Castle
Newark Castle
Whittington Castle
Norwich Castle
Ludlow Castle
Kenilworth Castle
Warwick Castle
St. Briavels Castle
Windsor Castle
The Tower of London
Allington Castle
Deal Castle
Dunster Castle
Farnham Castle
Bodiam Castle
Dover Castle
Hurstmonceux Castle
Pevensey Castle
Portchester Castle
Carisbrooke Castle
Corfe Castle
Restormel Castle
St. Michael's Mount

English Castles

Castles were introduced into Britain by the Normans. Earlier, the Romans and Britons had built camps and fortified places. It is thought that the Normans literally brought castles with them, as at that period they partly consisted of wooden palisades. The main feature was a large high mound, surrounded by a ditch, on top of which was built a wooden tower; the entrance was by a ramp or sloping bridge from an enclosure, or 'bailey', surrounded by a palisade and another ditch. These 'motte and bailey' castles were illustrated in the Bayeux Tapestry. One of the first in Britain, built soon after the Battle of Hastings, was probably at Berkhamsted, and hundreds were built as the Norman occupation spread – some of them only for temporary use.

The first stone castles date from about the same time; they were in use in Normandy in the eleventh century and the first few in England included the White Tower of the Tower of London and the Keep of Colchester Castle. As the wooden buildings were open to attack by fire, the use of stone was first for the main tower and the vulnerable entrances and later for the whole building.

Through the centuries the functions of the castle hardly changed – sometimes to protect particular routes at places such as river crossings, usually as a strong point to dominate the area and subdue the local population, often as a place of refuge. In the feudal system, castles showed the balance of power between different barons and between the barons and the king. The lord had to protect himself against possible attack from his followers as well as from external enemies, and comfort was often sacrificed to security.

The simplest structure for the safety of the lord's family was a tower with the entrance at first-floor level. These quarters were only used in time of siege, more comfortable apartments being built in the courtyard outside for use in quieter times. Later, more ambitious structures were used with strong towers or keeps, strong gatehouses to protect the entrances and curtain walls around the outside. As time went on, more attention was paid to the lord's private apartments, the chapel, garderobes (latrines), fireplaces, kitchens and hall.

The medieval methods of siege mainly consisted of the use of catapults and slings throwing stones, giant bows firing bolts, sapping underneath towers as well, of course, as more frontal assaults. These methods were not adequate against the strong stone keeps, the better curtain wall defences and the gatehouses strengthened by drawbridge, portcullis, murder holes and arrow slits until the use of firearms made the odds more even.

With the development of commerce arose the need to build town walls as a protection for the merchants, and later castles were used more as residences than as fortifications, although still laid out for defence. After the Wars of the Roses the residences of the nobility were houses rather than castles; the need for castles and forts shifted to the coasts. Henry VIII built many such defences round our southern shores in the sixteenth century.

Allington Castle

This restored Castle is Norman in origin, with alterations made later by the Wyatts. It lies on the River Medway near Maidstone and has a moat, curtain wall, great hall and gatehouse.

In its pleasant setting it shows the significance from the point of view of fortification of the battlements or crenellations. During the thirteenth century and later the King granted permission to loyal followers to fortify their residences in a 'licence to crenellate'.

In the Public Record Office is the licence of Edward I, with his Great Seal in green wax, written in Latin, of which the following is a translation:

'Edward by the grace of God King of England, Lord of Ireland and Duke of Aquitaine, to all to whom these letters come, greeting. Know that we have granted on behalf of ourselves and our heirs to our beloved and faithful Stephen of Penchester and Margaret his wife that they may fortify and crenellate their house at Allington in the county of Kent with a wall of stone and lime, and that they and their heirs may hold it, thus fortified and crenellated, for ever, without let or hindrance of us or our heirs or any of our officials. In witness whereof we have caused these our letters to be made patent. Witnessed by myself at Westminster on the twenty-third day of May in the ninth year of our reign.'

The Castle is now a Carmelite retreat house.

Bodiam Castle

The manor of Bodiam belonged to Sir Edward Dalyngrigge, who built the Castle under royal licence dated 1385 for the purpose of defending the area against possible attack by French naval forces up the River Rother, which was then navigable up to Bodiam Bridge. Successful attacks had already been made on Rye and Winchelsea.

But it was not until the Wars of the Roses that any active role was played by the Castle, and there is no evidence of any damage or serious attack during that period or during the Civil War.

The plan of the Castle is square, with high massive curtain walls with strong round towers at each corner, a square tower on two sides and two gatehouses on the other sides. The walls are 41 feet high and $6\frac{1}{2}$ feet thick; the towers over 60 feet high. Over the main gateway are the arms of the founder and other knights. Inside the court are arranged the hall, kitchen, staterooms, chapel, retainers' quarters, a dovecot and a well.

The moat is really a lake, and it is the approaches to the Castle from front and rear through the two gatehouses that are of special interest. Two massive square towers form the entrance to the Great Gatehouse. To reach the gatehouse involved first crossing a bridge from the edge of the moat, then a drawbridge on to a small stone octagon-shaped island, then a drawbridge to the barbican tower (which no longer exists) then over another drawbridge to the gatehouse. To add to the difficulties of attackers, the first bridge ran at right-angles to the second, so that the right sides of the attackers would be exposed, unprotected by the shield held in the left hand.

St. Michael's Mount

The rocky island has the sea for moat, except for the three or four hours of low tide.

At the time of the Domesday Book, there was a priory of Benedictine monks on the island, but nothing remains of the buildings; it continued to be a sanctuary, but its military value was recognised in 1194 by the appointment of a castellan.

After the Wars of the Roses, a Lancastrian exile, the Earl of Oxford, brought two ships from France to Mount's Bay, and with a small number of men took possession of the Mount in 1473 after entering disguised as pilgrims. There was no local support, but it took six months' siege to secure their surrender due to starvation, as even with artillery it was difficult to press home an effective attack.

A similar surprise gave the impostor Perkin Warbeck possession in 1497. He left his wife on the Mount with a small garrison, marched eastward and proclaimed himself king, but was forced to surrender at Beaulieu Abbey.

Again, in the Civil War it proved too difficult for a Parliamentary force under Colonel Hammond to overcome the defenders under Sir Francis Bassett, but it had to be evacuated after the King's surrender. On the Restoration, the Castle was returned to the Bassett family.

Up to this century a battery of six-pounders of eighteenth-century manufacture have stood on a plateau near the main entrance.

Corfe Castle

Corfe was the largest castle in Dorset, covering a conical hill in the only gap in the Purbeck Hills. There are traces of walls dating from before the Normans, but of the ruins now seen the keep and inner bailey that form the core of the Castle date from the early twelfth century.

Owing to its position on a narrow site on high ground, the Castle is roughly triangular; access was through the outer bailey via the outer gate, then the middle gate into the middle bailey from which the narrow inner gate gave access to the inner bailey. Both the outer gates included drawbridges and had two flanking towers. The important Buatavant Tower guarded the north and west flanks of the middle bailey. The square keep inside the inner bailey had two upper floors; the entrance was at first-floor level from an external staircase, protected by portcullis and forebuilding.

Like other castles, Corfe played its role at different times as a prison as well as undergoing siege. During the Civil War the Castle was slighted by the Parliamentarian forces after its capture in 1646, as was usual for them after a famous siege.

Bamburgh Castle

Bamburgh Castle site is spectacular. It is another of the border strongholds used for defence against the incursions of the Scots.

According to legend, this was the castle of Joyous Garde of Sir Launcelot, one of King Arthur's Round Table. This was the capital of Northumbria, and there was a wooden castle here before the Normans.

The keep was built in the reign of Henry I. After being damaged considerably in the Wars of the Roses the Castle was neglected but restored in part during the eighteenth century from a fund left by the Bishop of Durham, and the Bamburgh Trust still provides help in life-saving along that area of the coast.

A more complete restoration was carried out by Lord Armstrong at the end of the nineteenth century.

The Castle crowns a high basalt rock right at the edge of the sea. The south gate is guarded by flanking towers. The walls enclose 8 acres. The great keep stands at the inner bailey; it is made of small stones and the walls are 9–11 feet thick. In the basement is a well 150 feet deep that was in use in the eighth century and probably when an early castle was used for defence against the marauding Danes.

A ghost is said to haunt a narrow passage in the wall of the keep on the upper storey.

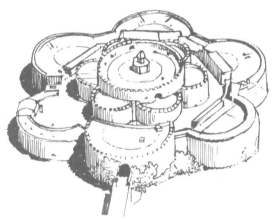

Deal Castle

Henry VIII was responsible for building coastal defences against possible invasion by the combined forces of France and the German Emperor, supported by the Pope. Deal was one of 'Three castles which keep the Downs', the other two being Sandwich and Walmer, which were completed about 1540. They came under the control of the Lord Warden of the Cinque Ports, and the first garrison consisted of thirty-four men and a Captain Thomas Wynkfelde of Sandwich.

The exposed faces of the fort were rounded in design to deflect shot. There are a total of 145 embrasures, or firing points, at five different levels to sweep every direction.

Little happened at the time of the Armada, and reports recorded the dilapidation of the Castle. Early in the Civil War these three forts were taken by Protestants, but they were surrendered to the Royalists after an uprising in Kent. The three castles were in turn besieged by Parliamentary troops and relieved by Royalist forces by sea, but besieged again and captured by Colonel Nathaniel Rich for Parliament in 1648.

The entrance has the original iron-studded oak door.

In the gatehouse is housed a museum of the archaeology of Deal and district.

Carisbrooke Castle

At Carisbrooke there is work of the Roman, medieval and Elizabethan periods. The outer earthworks are Roman. Over the gate at the entrance bridge are the initials of Queen Elizabeth I and the date 1598 when the outer lines of defence were started by an Italian engineer called Gianibelli. The Norman Castle after the Conquest was an island fortress and the lord of the Castle held the Isle of Wight; during the fourteenth century the Castle was attacked several times during French raids on the island.

King Charles was a prisoner here and the east bailey was laid out as a bowling-green for him. Two attempts to rescue him failed.

The Governor's house is now the Isle of Wight Museum.

After crossing the bridge over the moat, the gatehouse leads to the courtyard of the Castle, which, in addition to older buildings, contains a modern chapel, the remains of a two-storey building erected late in the sixteenth century by Sir George Carey to provide guest rooms, and the principal domestic buildings of different periods. In the north-east corner the keep stands on a great earthen mound which dates from the original Norman Castle; the tower is reached by climbing a long flight of steps up the mound.

In the south-east corner is a well with a wellhouse built in the sixteenth century, containing a large wooden tread-wheel worked by donkey power.

Dover Castle

Dover, chief of the Cinque Ports, was a port in Roman times – there is a Roman lighthouse.

The Norman keep of the Castle is one of the largest and possibly the finest example of a square keep. It was built between 1181 and 1187 by Henry II, and measures 98 feet by 96 feet at ground level and is 83 feet high, 95 feet to the tops of the square turrets; the walls are 22 feet thick at the base. The entrance is up a great staircase, protected by a forebuilding containing two chapels. Inside the keep is a well over 250 feet deep; lead pipes were used in a very unusual arrangement for the period to take water to different rooms.

The keep was protected by an inner line of ramparts and towers, and an outer line was added during the thirteenth century containing the Constable's Tower at the main entrance. In the period 1179 to 1191, records show a total of nearly £700 was spent on work on the Castle, probably under the supervision of a certain 'Maurice the Engineer'.

Dover Castle was held for King John against the besieging forces of rebel barons and their ally Prince Louis of France in 1216, in spite of efforts to starve the garrison and to mine under the walls by digging a trench.

Dunster Castle

This Castle has only changed hands once, except by inheritance, from Norman times to this century. In the Domesday Book, it said 'William of Mohun holds Torre and there is his castle'. The Mohuns were succeeded by the Luttrells in the fourteenth century.

The Castle rises from a curtain of woods above the river, the quaint little town acting as a foreground for the sylvan setting. The Tor was an obvious site to choose for a Norman castle. The top of the Tor is so steep that little work was needed to make the approach almost impossible, except up a path or steps. Later, a shell keep in stone was built on the top and a wall was run around the lower ward. All the buildings in normal use were within the outer bailey and there are no traces of buildings inside the shell keep on the summit.

In 1376 the male line of Mohuns died out and Dunster was sold to the Luttrell family. An imposing outer gatehouse was built about 1400; the gateway, which is about a century older, was more strongly fortified. The main front of the residential building was largely built by George Luttrell in 1589.

During the Civil War it was occupied by Royalists. It was besieged by Blake and bombarded by artillery placed in the town below, but the Governor, Colonel Wyndham, did not need to surrender until the Royalist cause had collapsed in the area.

An eighteenth-century Luttrell cleared the flat space at the top of the Tor and made a bowling-green there.

Hurstmonceux Castle

The need for fortress-castles ceased during the long reign of Edward III and few new ones were built except on the Scottish border. Many existing castles were allowed to become derelict or were used as gaols.

Castle-palaces were built instead, and Hurstmonceux is a magnificent large example, built in the 1440s from richly coloured medieval brick – one of the earliest in this material. This period represented the transition from Norman fortress to Tudor mansion. Although these fortified residences followed the form of the earlier castles in allowing for defence, much more attention was paid to comfort in planning the internal arrangements.

The entrance is the most ornate feature, piercing the lofty tower of the gatehouse; it has a quadrilateral plan, a broad moat and angle towers. But as a castle it was traditional rather than functional. The brickwork must have been easy to breach, and apart from the imposing appearance of the gatehouse the thin walls and slender towers and chimneys show that this was not a stronghold.

The Castle was restored in recent years and is now the home of the Royal Observatory, which was transferred here from Greenwich.

Farnham Castle

Farnham is one of the few castles in Surrey and stands on the River Wey.

It is an episcopal palace, recently the residence of the Bishop of Guildford, but for much longer the seat of the Bishop of Winchester.

The shell-keep remains. The earth mounds used previously made good positions for the first stone towers and they were usually built on top of the mound. In a few cases, of which Farnham and Berkeley are two, the shell-keep was built around the base of the mound.

This was the work of Bishop Henry de Blois between 1129 and 1171; it replaced an earlier central tower on top of the mound, which had been thrown down by order of King Henry II. He also built the original triangular bailey in which stands the Bishop's hall.

A later Bishop of Winchester, Waynflete, built the conspicuous corner tower of the bailey in the late fifteenth century and Bishop Fox (1500–1528) added to the keep.

The Castle fell into the hands of the French in 1216, but was recaptured the next year by the Earl of Pembroke. It was confiscated by Cromwell after changing hands twice during the Civil War, but was given back to the Bishop of Winchester after the Restoration.

It is now an overseas training college.

Kenilworth Castle

Kenilworth Castle is one of the finest in England and many famous names have been associated with it. It is said to have been built by Geoffrey de Clinton about 1120. The oldest building still standing is the strong Norman keep built between 1155 and 1170.

After it became a royal castle at the end of the twelfth century, King John and later King Henry III added curtain walls with towers and water defences in the form of a lake of 100 acres with outworks.

The Castle was the military headquarters of Simon de Montfort, and his son held out during a siege in 1266 that lasted most of the year. It was here that Edward II signed his abdication. John of Gaunt added the magnificent Great Hall and the private apartments, and what had been a castle became a palace.

The Dudleys held the Castle in the sixteenth century and here the Queen's favourite, the Earl of Leicester, entertained Elizabeth I lavishly. He modernised the keep, built a new north gatehouse and made other improvements.

During the Civil War the Castle changed hands twice and was slighted in 1649.

Lancaster Castle

There was a Roman fort near the River Lune, and when the Normans dispossessed the Saxon Earl Tostig the Castle was built by Roger of Poitou on Castle Hill, and the square stone tower later called Lungess Tower was built before 1102. Roger of Poitou was granted most of the area of Lancashire by the Conqueror and William II. The walls of the great keep are 10 feet thick.

King John visited the Castle in 1206 and it was strengthened during his reign, and there are records of repairs and expenses, including the enormous sum of £352. 3. 1 spent in 1210. King John's medieval castle, roughly circular, was about 365 feet in diameter, but little remains of it.

The raiding Scots were unable to take the Castle in several attacks during the fourteenth century, and although Robert Bruce burned Lancaster in 1322 the Castle, situated outside the town in those days, was unscathed.

Fifteenth-century additions were made to the gateway, known as John O'Gaunt Gateway, and carry the armorial shields of Henry IV and his son the Prince of Wales.

In 1643, the Castle was garrisoned by Parliament and the Earl of Derby with a Royalist army was unable to take the Castle but plundered the town. Some of the Castle defences were dismantled. In 1651, on the way south with his Scottish army, to be defeated at the Battle of Worcester, Prince Charles was proclaimed king in Lancaster.

The Tower of London

When the Tower of London was built at the side of the Thames by William the Conqueror, the purpose was to control as well as protect the city. At different times it has served as palace, fortress, arsenal and prison, and it has accommodated in its time the Royal Mint, the Public Records and the Royal Observatory.

The White Tower is the oldest building. It is 90 feet high and the walls are 15 feet thick at the base and 11 feet thick in the upper storey; the original entrance was on the first floor, reached by an external staircase as usual in such Norman castles for greater security. This keep has turrets at the four corners, square except the one at the north-east which is round.

The armouries contain a collection of armour attributable largely to the interest of Henry VIII and Charles II, and it is the oldest museum in England with specimens of all kinds of weapons, including early examples of breech loading, rifled barrels and revolvers. One suit of armour made for Henry VIII in the Greenwich royal workshops weighs 93 pounds.

Its many famous buildings include the Bloody Tower, so named because it is thought to have been the scene of the murder of Edward V and his brother, the Duke of York; Sir Walter Raleigh was imprisoned there. The Wakefield Tower houses the Crown jewels and regalia. On the river front is a collection of guns. The Traitor's Gate was useful as an entrance to the Tower when the Thames was used as a thoroughfare and served as a landing-place for prisoners after trial at Westminster.

Ludlow Castle

Although it is not clear who built it, Ludlow Castle was constructed to control this area of the Welsh borderland. It is first recorded in the possession of Joce de Dinan, a favourite knight of Henry I. The Castle was the scene of struggles between feuding barons and many of the sieges were unsuccessful, but it was taken once by Hugh de Lacy owing to treachery; Joce de Dinan besieged the Castle, but never regained possession. In the thirteenth century skirmishes with the Welsh under Llewelyn continued, in spite of a peace treaty signed by him with Henry III at Ludlow. Through the Wars of the Roses the Castle was held by the Yorkists, and Henry VI brought his army to Ludlow to attack Richard of York's stronghold; Richard's commander changed sides just before the battle and in the confusion the Lancastrians occupied the Castle. This loss was avenged by Richard's son Edward at the Battle of Mortimer's Cross nearby; Edward marched on London and declared himself king as Edward IV.

The Norman keep is the oldest part of the Castle; it was of four storeys and was 73 feet high; it guards the entrance to the inner court in the centre of which is the round Chapel of St. Mary Magdalene. On the north side are the main buildings, including the Solar or private apartments, the Great Hall or Council Chamber, the State apartments, the armoury and the apartment used by the two princes, sons of Edward IV, who were later murdered in the Tower of London.

It was in the Council Chamber that Milton's 'Comus' was first performed in 1634.

Newark Castle

Alexander, Bishop of Lincoln started the Castle about 1129. It was here that King John died in 1216, and it was visited by many English kings.

Newark was a strategic point on the old Roman ways from the south-west to the north and also from the east coast to the north, and it was still an important communications point at the time of the Civil War.

The gatehouse from the original Castle was built on three large arches, the centre one containing the doors; in the upper portion were the private apartments of the Bishop or Governor of the Castle, and on the other side was the chapel. The entrance from the River Trent was guarded by the Water Gate, which is of later date and equipped with a portcullis. There is an interesting fifteenth-century oriel window in the west wall.

Newark was a Royalist fortress throughout the Civil War; it was garrisoned in 1642 and until surrender in 1646 not only acted as a rallying point for the local Royalists, but also guarded the route from the north-east to the Royalist headquarters at Oxford, down which came supplies of arms bought in Holland. It also provided a possible base for the northern Royalist army to attack the south-east. Three attempts were made to take it by the Parliamentary forces. The last siege continued for six months, from November 1645 to May 1646, when, in spite of disease, the town and Castle only surrendered on instructions from the king.

Norwich Castle

Usually, castles in towns with defensive town walls are connected to the walls, probably at a corner. At Norwich and Newcastle, the Castle stands free in the walled area. However, the wall in the case of Norwich was built two centuries after the town had grown up around the Castle and Cathedral. The wall was begun in 1294 and completed in 1342 and the town enclosed was larger than any other in England.

The Domesday Book of 1086 records that 113 houses were demolished to make room for the Castle. The stone tower keep was built on the mound in the first half of the twelfth century, with a forebuilding for protection. The external ornament is unusual for this period.

East Anglia was an area in which the barons possessing castles struggled against the king in the revolt of Hugh Bigod in 1173 and against King John in 1216.

The Pipe Roll of 1193 shows that there was a garrison of seventy-five, including knights and men-at-arms both on horse and on foot. Its military importance was greater than the size of the garrison indicated (as was often the case).

Norwich was the administrative centre for both Norfolk and Suffolk when Henry II took possession on a pretext in 1157.

The Castle, now restored, houses a museum, and includes in the picture gallery examples of the 'Norwich school'.

Portchester Castle

A Roman road ran from London through Chichester to Portchester, and a stone fort was built there with ditches like the one at Richborough in Kent as a defence against the raids of Saxon pirates in the third century. Portchester was one of the largest of these forts, commanded by an officer with the title of 'Count of the Saxon Shore'. The tide still reaches the walls built by the Romans with hollow semi-circular bastions at intervals.

Inside the square Roman fort the north-west corner is now filled by the twelfth-century keep and extensive remains of the medieval castle, and the south-west corner by the beautiful twelfth-century church of an Augustinian priory – which is now the parish church.

During the twelfth century the early gatehouse was converted into a tower keep in two stages by blocking the entrance passage and adding additional storeys. The great Norman keep is 40 feet square at the base, where the walls are 8 feet thick. There are no fireplaces in the keep, which was intended for residence only in an emergency; other domestic buildings were put up against the walls. These were replaced at the same time as other work done in the fourteenth century, mainly during the reign of Richard II.

Portchester is an example of a low-lying coastal defence castle in its strategic position at the head of Portsmouth Harbour. It has always been a royal castle, with a Constable appointed by the Sovereign.

Pevensey Castle

It was at Pevensey that William the Conqueror landed, and it was not long before a Norman keep was added to what had been a Roman fort.

A series of forts were built by the Romans to resist Saxon raids from the sea between the Wash and Spithead. Unlike Portchester and Richborough, Pevensey is oval, not square, and its walls are reinforced with solid semi-circular bastions. The walls were mainly built of flint rubble and green sandstone held by courses of brick and ironstone. When Pevensey was besieged by King Stephen in 1147, it held out because of the strength of the old walls.

The Norman lord of the Castle was Richer de Aquila, who built a keep inside the large Roman fortress. Instead of the usual square Norman keep, it was irregular in shape and reinforced with projecting bastions. There were probably two reasons for building in stone – the site was rocky and also a strong defence was needed against possible invasion rather than simply local attacks.

The gatehouse and walls and the bastions of the inner bailey were added in the middle of the thirteenth century.

Restormel Castle

On the site of Restormel the first fortification was an earthwork, and the original masonry at the base of the gate tower dates from the early twelfth-century Norman castle built on the mound. There was an outer courtyard, of which little trace remains.

The Castle simply consists of the round keep on the mound, surrounded by a wide ditch. The walls are over 8 feet thick and the wall-walk is 25 feet above the courtyard inside. Against the inside of the wall is a series of apartments on the upper storey, while storerooms occupy the lower level. The entrance gate is a square tower set in the round curtain wall at the west, which had a drawbridge over the ditch and probably another inner drawbridge. Little now remains of the gate-tower.

In 1270 the Castle passed into the possession of Richard Earl of Cornwall, and after the death of his son who died in 1299 the Castle and the earldom reverted to the Crown. The title has since belonged to the monarch's eldest son. Edward the Black Prince visited the Castle in 1354 and 1365.

Scarborough Castle

Castle Rock is a natural stronghold, and traces of human occupation go back two and a half thousand years.

In Norman times the town passed into the hands of William le Gros, who built a castle on the headland, which he was forced to hand over to Henry II in 1155. The king improved the Castle between 1157 and 1164 at a cost of £532.

The site is triangular, overlooking the sea, about 300 feet above sea level, protected on the land side by a steep ravine – the Castle Dyke. The entrance was across a narrow neck of land, guarded on the outside by the barbican. Next, a central gatehouse tower was covered by a drawbridge on each side; the approach was then steeply uphill under the main curtain wall of the Castle and the keep.

In the Castle proper are three wards. The keep in the centre ward was 90 feet high; it had a basement and three upper floors. In case of trouble, the keep containing the residence of the constable or of the king when visiting the Castle could be defended against the rest of the Castle. The inner ward occupies most of the space on the site.

Before the Civil War, Scarborough was attacked many times through the centuries – for example, by the Scots in 1318 and Scots and French in 1378 from the sea. During the Civil War the commander changed sides and the siege of the Castle in 1645 by Parliamentary forces resulted in eventual surrender, due to disease and lack of water rather than the success of the bombardment from land and sea, although half the keep collapsed after intensive bombardment.

Warkworth Castle

This Castle stands at the neck of a peninsula where the River Coquet joins the sea, and contains buildings of several different centuries. It is an old stronghold of the Percy family, but was first a Saxon hall or castle. The first stone building dates back to Norman times.

The Earl of Northumberland, Hotspur's father, had to surrender after the Castle was damaged by the king's artillery. It suffered much damage, decay and depredations over the centuries.

From the south or landward side the curtain wall is entered through a frowning, magnificent gatehouse; the ditch was crossed by a drawbridge; the gatehouse is protected by all the strong defences available – machicolations above, the doors, gate, portcullis and loopholes on the flanks.

The great hall in the outer ward has a Norman fireplace. The entrance is by a porch below the Lion Tower, on which is the portrait of a lion, a collar with the Percy crescent and their motto 'Esperance'.

Elaborate planning was a feature of the keep, which is entered by steps up the mound. In the entrance is a trap in the form of a pit in the floor. Over the keep a slender lookout tower rises 32 feet above the roof, with a view of the river, the open sea and, over Central Northumberland, the distant Cheviot Hills.

Skipton Castle

Desormais, the word pierced in the parapet over the outer gatehouse – 'Henceforward' –
is the motto of the Cliffords.

Skipton commanded two Roman road junctions and the Aire Gap through the
Pennines. The lands were granted to Robert de Romille soon after Domesday, but his
Castle was probably not of stone, and a large part dates from Robert de Clifford between
1310 and 1314. The inner court, called the Conduit Court, resembled the Edwardian
castles in North Wales. It is six-sided in shape with strong round towers with walls
12 feet thick and about 40 feet in diameter.

The Cliffords played important parts in all the changes up to the Wars of the Roses,
when John the Black-faced (also known as 'Bloody Clifford') was killed by an arrow in
the throat in 1461. As there was so much merciless slaughter during the wars, not only
did his widow flee to Brough in Westmorland, but also handed over the heir – Henry,
aged eight – to the care of a shepherd, and it was not until Henry VII came to the throne
that the 'Shepherd Lord' emerged from his hiding place to take his estates.

During the Civil War, the Castle was eventually captured by Parliamentary forces
under Colonel Poyntz; the Castle had no water supply of its own and was dependent on
a pipeline which was cut. The Castle was slighted in 1648, except for a range of State
apartments which had been built in 1535. Restoration was carried out by Lady Anne
Clifford, Countess of Pembroke, in 1657 and 1658.

Warwick Castle

Warwick was one of the first Castles built by William the Conqueror to subdue the
country and the original earth mound can still be seen, on top of which the tower or
keep was later rebuilt.

During the fourteenth century, considerable rebuilding took place to strengthen the
military defences of the Castle, including the strong gatehouse with gates, portcullis and
two drawbridges with flanking towers on the town side, reinforced by a barbican. This
provided a defence system considered a masterpiece of military architecture of the
period. Caesar's Tower and Guy's Tower stand at either end of the gatehouse wall.
Caesar's Tower stands on a rock cliff rising up from the River Avon, and is itself
150 feet high; Guy's Tower is a little smaller.

Thomas Beauchamp built a great hall and other domestic apartments alongside the
river on the top of the cliff, on spacious and comfortable lines, so that the Castle also
assumed the proportions of a palace in the Gothic style. The whole Castle then consisted
of a single ward with four sides.

Of the castles not owned by the Crown, this is one of the most ambitious in design and
imposing in appearance.

St. Briavels Castle

Milo, Earl of Hereford, owned St. Briavels Castle in 1131, which is the earliest date on which it is recorded. In Norman times it was the administrative centre of the Forest of Dean.

Plantagenet kings stayed at the Castle when they enjoyed hunting wild boar and deer in the Forest, especially Henry II and John. The Constable of the Castle was also Warden of the Forest of Dean. St. Briavels was one of the centres for the manufacture of bolts for crossbows; for example, Henry III ordered 6,000 'quarrels' in 1223. The Constable was also instructed from time to time to supply miners, as well as archers, to work as sappers in mining under besieged castles such as Berwick in 1310-11.

There is a tradition that the villagers are given bread and cheese after evening service on Whit Sunday, and legend has it that this right was originally won for them by a Countess of Hereford in the same way that Lady Godiva rode through Coventry.

Little remains of the Norman keep but the entrance gateway and towers of the thirteenth century and walls of the twelfth century still stand. Other features are the prison, the kitchen with a spit-wheel turned by a dog, and the Constable's stone hunting horn fixed to a chimney in the Jury Room.

The Castle is now used as a youth hostel.

Windsor Castle

For over eight hundred years, Windsor Castle has been the chief residence of the Kings and Queens of England. Viewed from the River Thames, the Round Tower is seen to dominate the Castle, just as the Castle dominates the town. From among the massive pile of battlemented towers and terraces, St. George's Chapel and the Curfew Tower are outstanding.

The first Castle was begun by William the Conqueror and consisted of a keep surrounded by fortified walls. It was Henry I, his son, who started the building in stone, which was added to by many successive monarchs, especially Charles II.

St. George's Chapel was finished in 1528 and is the Chapel of the Knights of the Garter. The fan vaulting inside the roof is a famous feature of its Perpendicular style of architecture. The State Apartments contain many magnificent pieces of furniture and paintings, arms and armour.

Alnwick Castle

In 1309, Henry de Percy bought Alnwick. The Castle probably dated from the middle of the twelfth century, but it was as a Border stronghold against the Scots that it became of lasting importance.

After Edward II's defeat at Bannockburn, Northumberland was often overrun by the Scots, and indeed the border was fluid and ill-defined for two centuries. A garrison of 3,000 men-at-arms and some cavalry was needed to secure this stronghold. The most famous Percy was the Hotspur of Shakespeare's 'Henry IV', who killed 'some six or seven dozen of Scots at a breakfast'.

The barbican was built by the first Lord Percy. The outer defences at one time also included moat and drawbridge and iron gate; through the barbican, a portcullis and another tower. The Percy lion is over the doorway, and on the battlements are stone figures of men-at-arms. The exact purpose of these effigies is not clear, but as well as being decorative they certainly overawe in the dusk and must have done so in the conditions of an attack.

Famous features are Hotspur's Chair (a stone seat) and the Bloody Gap, later repaired, where a party of Scots broke through the wall, probably in 1327, and the story is that they were slain to a man.

The restoration of the Castle started in 1854 and is Italian in style. As well as relics and a library of 16,000 books, the Castle also contains canvases by Titian, Vandyck, Canaletto and Landseer.

Whittington Castle

The first Castle is reported to have been built here in 843 by Ynyr ap Cadfarch. In the Domesday Book it was called Wititone and the Castle belonged to the Peverils.

In 1083, Sir William Peveril offered his daughter Mellet, with Whittington, to the winner of a contest at his Castle in the Peak. The winner was Guarine de Retz from Alsace. The first son of the marriage was called Fulk Fitz-Warine, and the same first name was used by the male heirs for nine generations. This first Fulk Fitz-Warine married the daughter of the lord of Ludlow Castle, after saving her father's life.

The lords of the border areas, known as Marcher lords, were given special powers to help them defend the area against the incursions of the Welsh, and at one period the Welsh took possession of the Castle. There were many romantic and gallant episodes in the history of the successive Fulk Fitz-Warines, and the name is among those barons who forced the Magna Carta from King John.

The keep of the castle was fortified with five round towers, each 40 feet in diameter and 100 feet high, and the walls were 12 feet thick. During the seventeenth and eighteenth centuries, towers and walls fell down or were used to repair roads or to repair the outer gatehouse which is still standing with the remains of the moat in front of it.

Scottish Castles

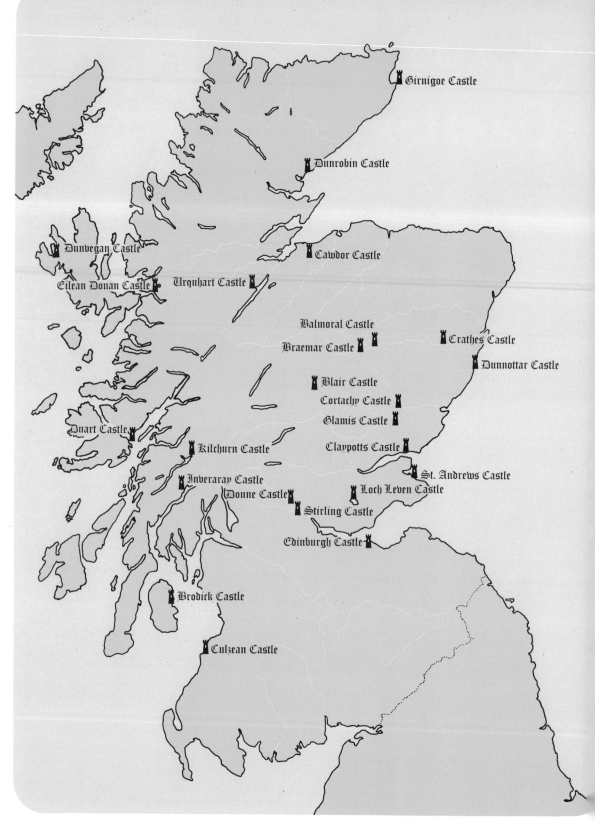

Girnigoe Castle

Dunrobin Castle

Dunvegan Castle

Cawdor Castle

Eilean Donan Castle   Urquhart Castle

Balmoral Castle

Braemar Castle   Crathes Castle

Dunnottar Castle

Blair Castle

Cortachy Castle

Glamis Castle

Duart Castle

Claypotts Castle

Kilchurn Castle

St. Andrews Castle

Inveraray Castle

Doune Castle   Loch Leven Castle

Stirling Castle

Edinburgh Castle

Brodick Castle

Culzean Castle

Scottish Castles

The castles of Scotland are its history in stone, ranging from the grandeur that is Edinburgh Castle to fortified dwellings of the Highland chiefs, to the border keeps of the Lowlands, to mansions built round more ancient fragments and to what sometimes is little more than out-size Victoriana.

A book of this size cannot hope fully to recount so much history but it can whet the appetite of the visitor to fill in for himself the gaps inevitably left by this brief account.

What may strike the visitor at once if he arrives from across the English border is the lack of anything to equal the great Norman castles of the south. Such castles did in fact exist but during the continuing struggles between Scotland and England the Scottish rulers found that they were so costly to hold or to regain that in a kind of scorched earth policy they tended to destroy them. A good example of this is Inverness which was destroyed on the orders of Robert the Bruce when he recaptured it in 1307. Over the centuries it was rebuilt but it was again completely destroyed by Prince Charlie after he had taken it in the 1745 rising. The present 'castle' still on the same site, is in fact an office block of Victorian origin.

Some of the castles have disappeared as if they had never been and only a Castle Street or Tower Road tells where they stood. For considerable parts of her history Scotland had a weak monarchy and the result was lawlessness among her nobles and chiefs so that almost every pass came to have its fortified house to guard the interests of a local baron and border castles had a lower chamber into which animals were herded while owners and followers fought from the rooms overhead. Other castles were royal hunting lodges and one or two belonged to the church and were fortified at the time of the Reformation.

Many of the castles which are still lived in are not open to the public though in the summer months it is worth while to find out locally if they are to be opened on behalf of a charity. Others, though occupied, are open regularly; some are in the care of the Government or of the National Trust for Scotland and are open to the public but the times are so divergent that it has not been possible to include the details here.

Balmoral Castle

The best known of all Deeside castles if of course, Balmoral, built by Queen Victoria and Prince Albert in the second half of the last century to designs in which the Prince Consort had a considerable personal hand. The original Balmoral Castle was first mentioned in the 15th century. Balmoral is in the midst of glorious countryside much loved by Queen Victoria and succeeding members of the Royal family, who come to Deeside every autumn. Except when the Royal family is in residence the gardens are open on weekdays during May, June and July.

Blair Castle

North of Blair Atholl is Blair Castle, home of the Duke of Atholl. It is a building of many periods begun in the 13th century. Comyn's Tower is the oldest part of the building. One of Cromwell's commanders stormed it in 1653; Claverhouse garrisoned it in 1689 and Prince Charles Edward stayed here during the '45. When the Castle had fallen into Hanoverian hands Lord George Murray had to besiege and damage his own home. Thirty rooms are now open to the public, portraying Scottish life over the last four centuries. The present medieval appearance of the exterior dates only from Victorian times, the original turrets and parapets having been torn down a hundred years before.

Braemar Castle

Braemar Castle, on Deeside, was built in 1628 by the Earl of Mar. Burned in 1689 it was largely re-built after the defeat of Bonnie Prince Charlie, the Young Pretender, at Culloden in 1746, and used as a barracks by Hanoverian troops ready to quell the still turbulent Highlanders. It was later acquired by the Farquharsons, who still own it. The eight-pointed curtain wall was added after the 1745 rebellion. Later still the turrets were heightened and battlemented. Inside the centre tower is a spiral staircase and below the ground level an old prison is still to be seen.

Brodick Castle

Castles on its islands helped guard the river Clyde. On Arran there were three castles at the end of the 16th century. The chief one, Brodick, is now the property of the National Trust for Scotland. On its site there was, it is believed, a Viking fort, the Lord of the Isles succeeding to it. Brodick was taken for Robert the Bruce from the English invaders in 1307. The castle came to Lord Boyd as part of the dowry of his bride Princess Mary, sister of James III. He was made Earl of Arran but the Boyd power did not last long and both title and castle became the property of James, Lord Hamilton, who married the widow. The castle was the centre of much feuding and was taken by Cromwell in 1652. The garrison were all later slain by the Earl of Arran and his men. The castle now contains a superb collection of paintings and furnishings and the gardens are outstanding.

Cawdor Castle

Six miles from Nairn is the magnificent Cawdor Castle, the site of which is said to have been chosen after a dream which told a Thane of Cawdor that he should build his house where a donkey lay down under a hawthorn tree! Alexander II gave the lands to the 1st Thane of Cawdor and the castle was built by the 5th Thane, the licence for its building by James II dated 1454 is still in existence. Shakespeare made this castle the scene of Duncan's murder by Macbeth.

The keep is the oldest part of the castle. Wings on the north and west sides were added in the 17th century. The moat and drawbridge are still there.

Claypotts Castle

Nothing remains of Dundee Castle. Of the other castles in and around the city Claypotts is the best preserved. Built between 1569 and 1588 it is a fine example of a fortified residence comprising a rectangular block with circular blocks butted on to it, topped by unusual gables. Sparsely decorated, it looks much more of a prison than a residence. The property is scheduled as an Ancient Monument. Broughty Ferry, where Claypotts is situated is now a residential suburb of Dundee. Its own castle was built about the same time as Claypotts and was once owned by 'Bonnie Dundee' the famous Scottish general.

Cortachy Castle

There is a belief that there was a castle at Cortachy in the 13th century which was used by King Robert the Bruce as a hunting lodge. Ogilvys had been in Cortachy since the 15th century and it was bought by the Airlie branch in the 17th century. Charles II stayed a night at Cortachy and in 1651 Cromwell's troops plundered it. Considerable additions and alterations have taken place over the years but the basis of the old castle remains although the total area is now more than double that of the original castle. Now occupied by Lord Airlie's son and heir, Lord Ogilvy, it is situated about 3 miles north of Kirriemuir in Angus.

Crathes Castle

Crathes Castle and its fine gardens are now in the care of the National Trust for Scotland. It had been occupied by the same family, the Burnetts of Leys, since the castle, with its turrets and battlements, was built in the 16th century. When King Robert the Bruce gave the Burnetts the Charter for the land of Leys in 1323 he is said to have given also the ivory Horn of Leys which must never leave the castle. The fine painted ceilings are 16th century and several pieces of furniture also date from this period. The gardens, first laid out in the 18th century are of absorbing interest being divided up into separate units by the massive old yew hedges.

Culzean Castle

Culzean Castle, near Maybole in Ayrshire, overlooks the Firth of Clyde. Designed by Robert Adam in the late 18th century for the Earl of Cassilis, it incorporates part of an original Kennedy stronghold. Now in the care of the National Trust for Scotland it is indeed a magnificent structure and among its outstanding features are the glorious staircase, plaster ceilings and a round drawing room. The suite of rooms preserved for the late General Eisenhower in 1946 to be used as his Scottish residence attracts large numbers of visitors, as do the beautifully kept gardens and surrounding woodlands.

Doune Castle

Doune Castle with its fine twin towers stands above the junction of two rivers just below the Perthshire town of Doune. Robert, Duke of Albany, probably built most of the castle around the end of the 14th century. He and his son Murdoch were regents during the long captivity of James I. The castle was later forfeited to the crown and James IV gave it to his queen and it eventually went to her third husband Lord Methven. It was the home of The Bonnie Earl of Moray of ballad fame who was murdered in 1592. A nephew of Rob Roy garrisoned it for Prince Charles Edward.

Duart Castle

Well known to all who sail westwards from Oban is Duart Castle on the island of Mull, home of the chief of the Clan Maclean. After long being a ruin it was restored this century by Sir Fitzroy Maclean, 10th baronet. Parts of the building may date from the 13th century. In 1588 Sir Lachlan Maclean received the surrender of the Spanish galleon *Florencia*, a survivor of the Armada, but disagreements ended in the blowing up of the galleon in Tobermory Bay. The ship's captain was held a prisoner in the castle. For his support of the Stuarts in 1745 Sir Hector Maclean of Duart was imprisoned in the Tower of London and later went into exile.

Dunnottar Castle

The impressive ruin of Dunnottar Castle, 2 miles south of Stonehaven, is perched on a rocky headland 160 feet above the North Sea. It was begun in the 14th century by the Great Marischal of Scotland. The walls of the original rectangular keep are five feet thick and 50 feet high. The castle, to which additions were made during the 15th, 16th and 17th centuries, was besieged by Cromwell's troops for eight months before it fell in 1652. The crown, sceptre and sword of Scotland, which had been hidden in the castle, were smuggled away before the castle capitulated. Visitors can still see the dungeon known as the 'Whig's Vault' in which more than a hundred Covenanters were imprisoned in 1685.

Dunrobin Castle

Now in part a boarding school for boys, Dunrobin Castle, in eastern Sutherlandshire, stands in a dominating position near the village of Golspie. There was a fortified building here in the 12th century but the earliest part of the present building may not date earlier than the beginning of the 15th century. It has been famous over the centuries as the chief seat of the powerful Sutherland family. The first Earl of Sutherland, created in 1235, was a descendant of Hugh Freskin who had been granted land in Sutherland by William the Lion. The present gardens are magnificent and there is an interesting museum in the grounds.

Dunvegan Castle

Turning now to the Isle of Skye, the best known of its castles is of course Dunvegan, seat of the chiefs of Macleod. Rising straight from a rock above the shore its origins are lost in legend but the present castle includes 13th, 14th and 15th century building. Johnston and Boswell stayed here on their Hebridean journey and in the castle are preserved the Fairy Flag given to the 4th chief in the 14th century and the drinking horn of the 16th chief. Visitors can see some fine paintings and also pipes belonging to the Macrimmons, hereditary pipers to the Macleods. There is also a fearsome bottle dungeon.

Edinburgh Castle

The natural place to start our tour of Scottish castles seems surely to be at the greatest of them all – Edinburgh, perched high above Princes Street Gardens. It links the ancient with the newest at its annual tattoo when, floodlit, it seems to float in the dark sky. There was a castle here in Pictish times but it is from the 11th century that we know its full history. One of the oldest ecclesiastical buildings in the land is its St. Margaret Chapel. Margaret was the saintly wife of Malcolm Canmore and she died in Edinburgh in 1093. This, the only Norman work in the city, was restored in the 19th century.

The castle figured in many wars and was dismantled by Bruce after it had been taken from the English in 1313 by a daring climb up the southern face by the Earl of Moray. It was later given to the English by Edward Balliol but after Edward III had refortified it, the Scots once more recaptured it and it was then greatly strengthened. James VI of Scotland, 1st of England was born here and the castle held out desparately for Mary Queen of Scots. It was besieged by Cromwell and refused to welcome Prince Charles Stuart in 1745.

Eilean Donan Castle

A focal point set in magnificent scenery is Eilean Donan Castle at the mouth of Loch Duich near Dornie in Ross and Cromarty, where a Caledonian vitrified fort once stood. It could not have anything but a stirring history in such a position. Fifty heads decorated its walls as a warning from the Earl of Moray in the 14th century. Spanish troops under the Earl of Seaforth held it during a hopeless Jacobite rising in 1719 and as a result it was bombarded and largely destroyed by three English ships. It was splendidly restored during the earlier part of the present century.

Girnigoe Castle

The Caithness castles perched on the eastern cliffs are spectacular in the extreme and none more so than the oddly named Girnigoe. Like most of the Caithness castles it was a Sinclair stronghold. In 1455 William Sinclair, 3rd Earl of Orkney, was forced to resign an earldom held from the King of Denmark and James III made him Earl of Caithness. A son built Girnigoe which shared its rocky peninsula at Noss Head with the later castle Sinclair. The 4th Earl was chairman of the jury that aquitted Bothwell of Darnley's murder and was a staunch supporter of Mary Queen of Scots.

Glamis Castle

Twelve miles to the north of Dundee is one of the best known of all Scottish Castles. Glamis is open to the public certain days a week and can be seen from a viewpoint on the Glamis to Kirriemuir road. Its owner is the Earl of Strathmore, a cousin of the Queen: it was a childhood home of the Queen Mother and in it Princess Margaret was born. There has been a castle at Glamis since ancient times and there is a belief that King Malcolm II was murdered here. The oldest part of the present building dates from the 14th century. In 1372 Sir John Lyon married a daughter of King Robert II and was made Thane of Glamis. The building, which has been much added to, is reminiscent of a French Chateau.

Inveraray Castle

The original home of the Campbells of Argyll was at Innischonnel Castle on a small island on the eastern side of Loch Awe. Their present castle at Inveraray was built originally about 1520. It was replanned and rebuilt during the 18th century, finished in 1770 and by 1773 all trace of the earlier castle had been removed. The interior is a veritable treasure house of 18th century and earlier furniture and works of art set out in rooms of outstanding elegance. There is also an outstandingly interesting collection of early Scottish weapons. The interior is open to the public at advertised times.

Kilchurn Castle

Kilchurn Castle, in Argyllshire is an imposing ruin standing in wonderful scenery at the head of Loch Awe to the west of Dalmally. It was built about the middle of the 15th century, with additions on the north and south sides during the 16th and 17th centuries. The site at the time of the original building was an island but is now surrounded by marshy ground. This was originally MacGregor country but when that clan fell the castle came into the hands of Sir Duncan Campbell of Lochow and passed to his younger son. It was added to by a descendant, 'Duncan of the Seven Castles', some hundred years later.

Loch Leven Castle

Loch Leven Castle, now in ruins, stands on an island in the loch about a mile from Kinross. It was unsuccessfully besieged by the English at the beginning of the 14th century. The lands had come into the Douglas family about that time and though there were prisoners in it before and after her, Mary Queen of Scots and her escape is what is remembered. The infamous Douglas, the Earl of Morton, consigned her there in June 1567 and she was forced to sign a deed of abdication in favour of her infant son. After one unsuccessful attempt she escaped in May the next year with the aid of a youth, Willy Douglas, who had stolen the keys. He let her and her serving woman free, locked the door again and threw the keys into the loch. Waiting for them were Lord Seton and other faithful followers.

St. Andrews Castle

Of course the great castle in Fife was St. Andrews. Jutting out into the sea, its ruins still giving an atmosphere of grandeur and strength which add to the unique charm of this University town. It is claimed that the original building, built in the 13th century, was an Episcopal residence and the oldest parts of the ruins date from around that time. Among the castle's interesting features are the grim bottle dungeon and the well. It seems from the first to have been of military importance and Edward Balliol took the castle and held it for four years before it was recovered for David II by Sir Andrew Moray of Bothwell who dismantled it. A new building rose again and James III would appear to have been born in it and it was there that James V greeted Mary of Guise on her arrival from France. In the 16th century, during a dispute over the succession to the archbishopric, the castle was taken and retaken as intrigue followed intrigue. The most famous, or infamous, of the churchmen were James Beaton and his nephew and successor Cardinal Beaton. They had immense power, taking precedence after the Royal family. Heretics were burned in the streets of St. Andrews some for thinly veiled political motives. Cardinal Beaton was in power from 1539 to his death in 1546. Like his uncle, he took part in many tortuous plots and from the castle in 1545 he watched the burning at the stake of the preacher George Wishart. As a speedy result he was killed by a number of Wishart's friends led by Norman Leslie, eldest son of the Earl of Rothes. The Reformers held the Castle till the following year when it was taken by French troops. Many of the prisoners, including John Knox, were carried off to France to be galley slaves. James VI found refuge here after the Raid of Ruthven. Later the castle passed into the keeping of the town, but there are records of them using it as a kind of quarry to repair such things as the pier in the 17th century!

Stirling Castle

Stirling Castle provides a most wonderful vantage point with views over central Scotland and the sites of many battles. It was a fortress and a royal palace and its buildings were often destroyed and rebuilt or reshaped as fashion demanded. Still surviving, however, is the 15th century hall built by James III; the Royal Palace, much of which was fashioned at the command of James V, and the Chapel Royal built by James VI on the site of an earlier one. The history of the Castle would fill a volume as for centuries it was among the most important in the land. Alexander I died in the castle in 1124, as did William the Lion. It was a favourite Royal residence and legend has it that Alexander II was in residence when he established trial by jury as law. So strong was the castle that Edward I by-passed it and did not attack it until all other towns had surrendered to him. It took a three months siege to capture it. Stirling throughout the centuries was a place of refuge for many of the Royal family in danger from their own subjects. It is still garrisoned but a part is open to the public.

Urquhart Castle

On Loch Ness near Drumnadrochit are the extensive ruins of Urquhart Castle which was one of the largest castles in Scotland. A fortification stood there from earliest times and part of the present ruin dates from the 13th century. It figured largely in the struggles against the English from the time of William Wallace and was besieged, taken and retaken many times. Robert Chisholm, a Roxburgh laird, was made Sheriff of Inverness and constable of the Royal Castle of Urquhart in the 14th century. The Chisholms settled in the Highlands and became a highland clan. Their stronghold was Erchless Castle in the remoteness of Strathglass and in both the 1715 and the 1745 risings they fought for the Stuarts.

Welsh
Castles

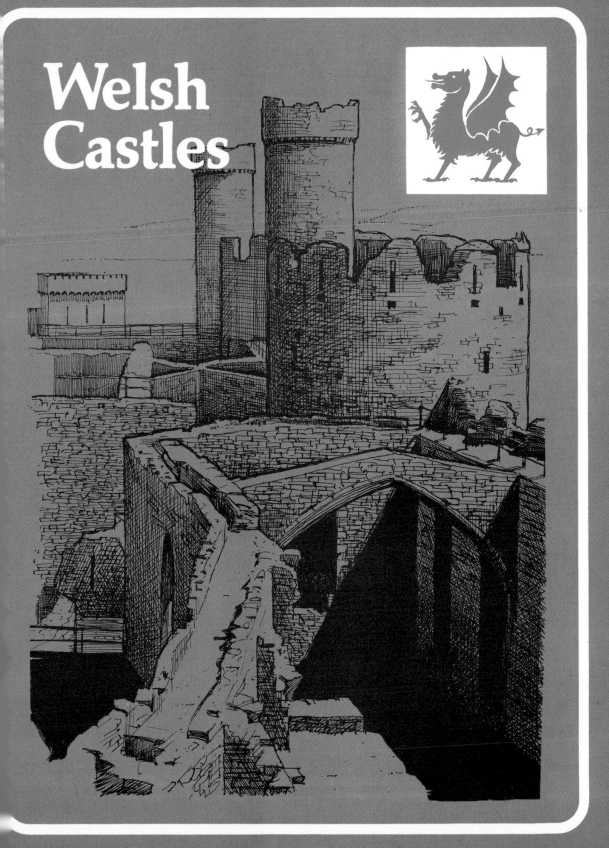

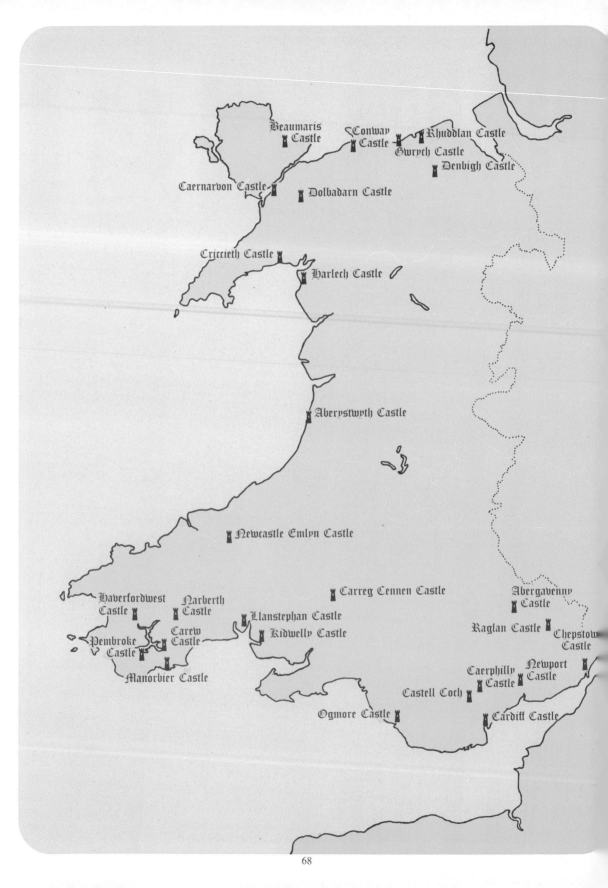

Welsh Castles

In addition to its magnificent mountain and coastal scenery, forests and beaches, Wales boasts a wealth of castles that attract visitors from far and near.

It was the feudal system that created castles, which were the private fortresses of the king and of the nobles. This system was based on service in exchange for land and in turn this led to quarrels between neighbours so that protection was needed. The castles in England were built mainly by the Norman nobles to implement this system by defending the land they had been granted, or had taken, and to suppress the local population as well as to guard strategic points. This defence system was imposed later on Wales and Ireland.

In earlier times there were forts and fortified camps and there are traces of Roman camps in Wales as well as the hill top sites of ancient British forts. When the Normans pushed into Wales in the 11th and 12th centuries the usual type of castle consisted of a mound of earth, a palissade and a ditch. They were easily made and often not permanent residences and stone castles were soon introduced, also by the Normans, partly depending on the availability of local stone.

During the 12th century the Welsh princes of North Wales were given the opportunity to increase their power and they built stone castles such as those at Criccieth and Dolbadarn. The mountains in South Wales also impeded the Norman progress and the hills contained the strongholds of the Welsh.

Meanwhile the Marcher lords built themselves castles on the borders of Wales both to keep the Welsh out and as bases for their own invasions of the country.

Another type of castle was built in the North by Edward I in his long campaign against Llewelyn at the end of the 13th century. Some, like Denbigh, Harlech and Caernarvon were captured by the Welsh at times in the course of the struggle. They were built to control communications from the sea and through the valleys and the remains are in splendid condition today.

Town walls were joined to the castles as a complete system of defence at Caernarvon and Denbigh, while Conway is a particularly impressive example of the idea of including settlements to extend the English control of the area.

These castles are magnificent examples of military architecture. Beaumaris is the most superb of all in the plan, which is worked out in extreme detail of outer and inner defence systems. It is set alongside the sea at the northern end of the Menai Straits, which are guarded at the southern end by Caernarvon.

The visitor cannot fail to be impressed by the size of the castles built in the reign of Edward I; they represented an ambitious building programme at enormous expense. During the year 1295 Beaumaris employed four hundred masons, thirty smiths and carpenters, one thousand labourers and two hundred carters. In the year 1291 Caernarvon, Conway and Harlech cost the king over £14,000 – an enormous sum in those days.

Caerphilly in South Wales is another example of the concentric system of defence; including the use of water it is the largest in Wales. Raglan is a superb example of 15th century building. In South Wales there is an excellent specimen of the castle and walled town system in Chepstow, set at the mouth of the River Wye.

Abergavenny Castle

Abergavenny's Castle is now a ruin standing on the wooded hill that dominates the town. All that is visible is the gatehouse, the mound, some of the walls and the foundations of the keep.

The importance of the position of the castle is that it stands on the edge of the hills where the Rivers Usk and Gavenny join. It was a Roman site, and one of the early Norman castles was built there about 1100.

William de Braose inherited Abergavenny in 1177 and was infamous in Welsh history for his treachery. Seisyll, a Welsh prince, and other Welsh notables of the Gwent district were invited to a banquet and all were killed at the table. The Welsh later captured the castle but it was not until thirty years later that justice was done to de Braose by King John depriving him of his lands and he died a beggar.

Llewelyn captured the castle in 1215 and it was again taken by the Welsh under Owen Glendower in 1403 and burned. During the Civil War it was captured by Fairfax and slighted. No doubt a lot of the remaining masonry was 'robbed' for building in the town.

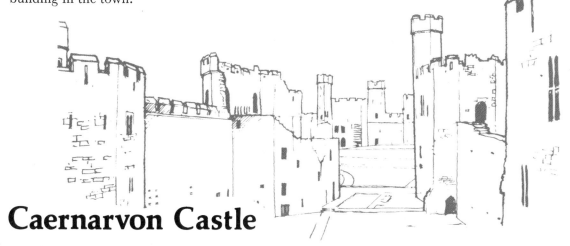

Caernarvon Castle

Caernarvon Castle was begun in 1285 after Edward I's successful campaign against the Welsh. It is interesting to note that the quay and the town walls were completed before the construction of the moated castle was commenced These steps were taken to safeguard communications by sea and to ensure protection for the English settlers. The ground plan of the castle shows two roughly circular areas connected by a narrow neck – rather like a figure of eight or an hour glass – the Outer Bailey containing the King's Gate and the Inner Bailey containing the Eagle Tower. In all there are two double gatehouses and nine towers and yet a garrison of 40 men could defend the whole castle.

Thought by many to be the most magnificent of the Edwardian Welsh castles, Caernarvon was the birthplace of Edward II, the first Prince of Wales, and it was he who finally completed the castle in 1327.

The castle withstood attacks from Owen Glendower, the last of the Welsh princes, and, in 1404, from the French but after changing hands during the Civil War it fell into ruin, narrowly escaping demolition on the orders of Charles II. Its restoration to the condition it is in today took place little over a hundred years ago.

Beaumaris Castle

The castle does not have the grandeur of some of the bigger castles built by Edward I but it is a classic example of the concentric castle, with every feature planned for defence in symmetrical form. The main principle of the design was that any enemy gaining control of the outer curtain would be left at the mercy of the garrison in the inner ward.

As there were no limitations imposed by the site the design is most attractive. It was the most advanced of the group of castles in North Wales and included a sea-water moat and a dock for shipping protected by the outer defences of the castle. The Welsh under Madoc had captured Caernarvon, the greatest of Edward's castles, in 1294 and work was started on Beaumaris to guard the Menai Straits in 1295 and the work was put in hand speedily with a large labour force using stone from Penmon. It was not completed until 1323. It was never attacked.

The garrison consisted of ten men-at-arms, twenty crossbow men and a hundred foot soldiers. Records show that £7,000 (equal to three-quarters of a million pounds today) had been spent in 1298. So far as the masonry goes it remains very much as it was in the 14th century and the visitor therefore has a good picture of what it was like when small ships could sail up to the castle and tie up at Gunner's Walk.

Aberystwyth Castle

All that remains of Aberystwyth Castle today is a tower on a steep hill at the end of the promenade, a pleasant place with views over the sea. Of 12th and 13th century origins it was once a link in the chain of Edwardian fortresses placed at strategic points to control North Wales.

Records exist of an early castle built in 1110 by Gilbert FitzRichard, one of the many of earth and timber built to control areas occupied by the Normans. It was burned several times by the Welsh before being rebuilt in stone by Edward I.

James of St. George, the master mason who built Aberystwyth for Edward I, had several assistants from Savoy, where he gained his experience. Like the other North Wales castles, Aberystwyth could be supplied from the sea, and it had a town built alongside it as a colony for English settlers.

The plan at Aberystwyth was of a symmetrical castle without a keep, defended by two lines of walls, both diamond-shaped in plan, and a moat. The inner curtain had a large gatehouse at one corner and round towers at the others.

During the rebellion of Owen Glendower it was one of his headquarters from 1404–8. It was then recaptured by Henry of Monmouth (later Henry V) with the aid of the 'King's Gun' weighing four and a half tons which was brought over from Nottingham for the assault.

After the Civil War the castle was mined and blown up by Cromwell's troops.

Caerphilly Castle

Caerphilly is the largest Welsh castle in overall size and must have been a striking sight when the towers seemed to rise straight out of the lakes that defended it. The lakes have now been drained. The castle was built on the concentric plan by Gilbert, Earl of Gloucester, in 1267.

Llewelyn of Gwynedd descended on the building soon after it was started and demolished it, but Gilbert de Clare, known as the Red Earl, persisted in the construction of a very ambitious fortress.

The inner ward is defended by two gatehouses and four corner towers which all stood high above the outer ward. This in turn was protected by lakes which were made by damming up two streams. Where a bridge crossed over the lake on the eastern side was a strong barbican and moat to guard the main entrance. Another entrance was by boat to a small island or 'hornwork' on the western side of the lake from which passage could be had over a drawbridge into the outer ward on the main island.

The visitor can see how heavily these entrances were guarded by the interdependent towers of the outer and inner gatehouses.

Caerphilly was so strong that it was not taken by assault although the outer ward was surprised and burned by Llewelyn Bren in 1315. Gunpowder was used to slight it after the Civil War, and left the 'leaning tower', a curious sight for visitors.

Carreg Cennen Castle

Dramatically and picturesquely situated, the castle stands on a limestone crag about three hundred feet above the valley, separated from the hills by the River Cennen.

The buildings date mainly from the 13th and early 14th centuries. Inside the upper half of the outer ward is a lime kiln used for making mortar. Nearby is a passage that leads to steps on the edge of the cliff that go down into a long narrow cave which includes a dovecote and a small water supply. Between the outer and inner wards is a strong and elaborate barbican. The passage to the inner ward lay over three drawbridges.

The inner ward was protected by ditches and the cliffs, with the entrance guarded by the gatehouse with two strong towers which have arrow slits. On the eastern side of the inner ward the living quarters are on the first floor – kitchen, hall and private apartments. The chapel was reached by stairs leading up from the hall inside the wall and was situated in a tower overlooking the upper half of the outer ward. It, too, was provided with arrow slits.

Most of the re-building of this originally Welsh fortress was done by John Giffard, to whom Edward I granted the castle in 1283. After being taken by the Yorkists in the Wars of the Roses it was demolished by Edward IV in 1462.

Cardiff Castle

The Normans first reached Glamorgan by sea and their leader, FitzHamon, built a castle at Cardiff about 1093 on the site of the old Roman fort. This is the finest example in Wales of a Norman castle on a mound surrounded by a ditch. Visitors to Cardiff can see the position very clearly but the mound is now crowned by a shell keep of stone, dating from the 13th century.

In one of the early buildings on the mound Henry I kept his brother Robert of Normandy captive. From here Ivor Bach of Senghenydd, one of the minor Welsh chiefs, carried off Earl William of Gloucester and his wife and son in 1158 after entering the keep by a ladder.

Each family extended the castle. Many of the older buildings were built during the ownership of the de Clares who built the Black Tower of Glamorgan as the south front gatehouse. Cardiff, as the head of the lordship of Glamorgan, changed hands many times until it was given to Jasper Tudor and became part of the royal domain.

After the Act of Union of 1536 the medieval importance of Cardiff castle ceased and there was no reason for the Crown to keep possession. During the Civil War it changed hands twice but was not slighted.

There have been numerous alterations in modern times including some in neo-Gothic style.

Castell Coch (Red Castle)

The first Welsh residence of the princess of Powys was on a mound a short distance away from the present castle. The first stone fortress was built before 1216 and was occupied by Gruffyd ap Gwenwynym.

The princes of southern Powys at Castell Coch were traditionally allies of the English as they were rivals of the princes of Gwynedd. Castell Coch belonged to Welsh owners throughout the 13th century and they attended Edward I's parliaments as English barons.

Under the English law of succession the castle and lands passed into the Cherlton family of marcher barons after the end of the male line by the decision of Edward II. When a similar situation arose in 1422 the castle was shared between the Greys and the Tiptofts and in 1540 it is recorded that the Tiptoft part was 'almost fallen down' and the Greys finally bought out the other half.

The estate was sold to the Herberts of Pembroke and still later passed into the hands of the family of Clive of Plassey.

Originally of triangular plan with round towers at the corners, the castle, now scheduled as an ancient monument, has been considerably restored.

Chepstow Castle

Chepstow is three miles from the mouth of the River Wye on rising ground on the west bank. It is a town of history – in the past a castle, a market town and a port. For defence it was bounded on two sides by the town wall, the river and the castle forming the other two.

Chepstow Castle, one of the mightiest Norman strongholds in the west, was started in 1067 by William FitzOsbern who was a follower of William the Conqueror. It was rebuilt and extended later by Roger Bigod, the fifth Earl of Norfolk. The fine keep dates partly from the 11th century while most of the existing building goes back to the 13th century. It consists of a series of courts following the contours of the cliff.

The four courtyards are overlooked by the hall keep which is forty feet high, and round towers strengthen the thick curtain walls. Two massive gatehouses cover the entrances at front and rear. The bridge over the River Wye and the town gate were the only entrances through the wall in medieval times. The castle is now in the care of the Department of the Environment, like many other historic places in the Wye Valley. A good view is to be had from the iron bridge across the Wye at the bottom of the town.

Conway Castle

This magnificent fortress is another outstanding example of Edward I's genius for military architecture. Its original plan was triangular, with a round tower at the western end but this was amended and the visitor now sees eight massive drum towers and curtain walls some fifteen feet thick. Built as a residence as well as a fortress, Queen Eleanor was able to stay at Conway with Edward I on a number of occasions. The castle was sited on a broad, precipitous rock by the side of the Conway river and the Gyffin brook. Conway itself, like Caernarvon, was a walled town with, originally, a total of 27 defence towers.

At the eastern end of the castle a water gate leads to a barbican while at the western end there is a forecourt and barbican for the entrance from the town. There is no strong keep or gatehouse but there are an inner ward and an outer ward protected by the eight towers and massive curtain walls mentioned above and all in a good state of preservation.

Criccieth Castle

Criccieth was originally a Welsh castle and there is a record of it going back to 1239.

When Edward I conquered North Wales he held the country by building strong new castles and re-building old ones. Criccieth was one of the Welsh castles that were strengthened. As only £306 was spent on it in 1292, compared with sums like £8,000 on the new castles of Harlech, Conway and Caernarvon, the work done was evidently small.

When, in 1284, Edward appointed William de Leyburn as Constable the garrison was thirty men and he was paid £100 a year.

It is a simple castle with an unusual layout owing to the shape of the site and its position. The Inner Ward dates from the original building in the early 13th century. The Outer Ward is protected by the Leyburn Tower, a curtain wall, and the Engine Tower which were built later in the 13th century. The tower named after the Constable was evidently an impressive residence; the other had a platform for a stone-throwing engine and the ammunition had to be hauled up shallow steps.

Denbigh Castle

The original Welsh castle, a timber building on top of a mound, was the residence of Dafydd ap Gruffydd the brother of Llewelyn. In Edward I's successful campaign of 1282 it withstood attack for a period but after its capture it was replaced by a stone castle built between 1282 and 1322 by de Lacey, Earl of Lincoln. In the case of places where towns were to be settled in North Wales by Edward I it was usual to build the town walls first, while making use of the existing castle for defence, and then to build a new castle within the ring of outer defences, in this case in the highest and least accessible part of the town.

'Hotspur' – Henry Percy – used it as his headquarters in 1399 and the town was burned by Owen Glendower in 1402. The town was again burned in 1468 when Jasper Tudor, Earl of Pembroke, captured the castle from the Yorkists after a siege. The town of Denbigh was then removed to a site outside the walls.

The gatehouse is the most impressive feature of the second stage of building. The approach was over a ditch thirty feet wide protected by drawbridge, portcullises, and murder holes. Three octagonal towers form the gatehouse enclosing an octagonal hall. The entrance passage has a fine arch above which the visitor will see one of the original three panels holding a figure alleged to be of Edward I.

Dolbadarn Castle

When North Wales was raided by Norsemen and Danes the men of Gwynedd retreated to the wildest and strongest places they had. The stone castles and strongholds they built in these inaccessible positions date from before the sophisticated military architecture of the English castles built by Edward I at the end of the 13th century.

Dolbadarn Castle stands between the two lakes Peris and Padarn near the Llanberis pass and occupies a very narrow platform of rock with steep slopes around the sides. It is 13th century Welsh construction and it is recorded that after a battle at Bryn Derwin in 1255, Llewelyn ap Gruffydd imprisoned his brother Owain in the castle.

The principal tower was the main means of defence; the entrance to it was on the first floor and its defences included a portcullis. The lower floor could be reached probably only by a trap door from the first floor. Both the round keep and the outer courtyard walls and square towers were made of local grit and slate. Records show that the tower was partly dismantled in the reign of Edward I when timbers were removed to Caernarvon in 1284.

Gwrych Castle

The visitor to Abergele will find that to the west of the town the hills begin to come nearer to the sea. About half a mile away, at the foot of these wooded slopes and alongside the old main road is Gwrych Castle which was at one time the home of the Earl of Dundonald who became famous as a soldier in the South African War.

Gwrych is an imposing mock antique built in 1815 and should be enjoyed by the visitor in the spirit in which it was built. Several of its towers are sham. The castle contains some magnificent furniture, a splendid great hall, and oak panelling, ceilings and staircase of considerable interest. Inscribed on tablets outside the castle is a list of some of the more important historic events which have taken place in the district.

It was at the village of Llandulas nearby that the Earl of Northumberland led Richard II into ambush and capture after Richard came back to Conway from Ireland.

Harlech Castle

The sea used to reach the foot of the rock that is the base of this massive and magnificent castle built by Edward I. Records show that the building started in 1285 when £205 was spent on cutting the ditch out of the rock in front of the castle. Between 1286 and 1290 nearly £8,000 was spent on masonry work for the towers, gatehouse and curtain walls.

When the castle was besieged by Madoc ap Llewelyn in 1294–5 it held out with a garrison of thirty-seven men. It was captured in 1404 by Owen Glendower in the rebellion he started in 1400. He obtained control of almost all North Wales and used Harlech as his headquarters and capital.

During the Wars of the Roses it was the last stronghold to be handed over to the Yorkists. It later decayed but was used again during the Civil War and was the last of the North Wales castles to fall to the Parliamentarians.

The entrance over the moat was across a stone arch and over two drawbridges protected by a barbican or outer gatehouse. The great strength of the castle is the main gatehouse which dominates it and has three storeys. The entrance itself is guarded by portcullises, doors and arrow slits along the length of the passage.

Visitors can reach the top of the four towers at the corners of the inner ward giving beautiful views over Snowdonia, Tremadoc Bay and the Lleyn peninsula.

Kidwelly Castle

This is one of a series of Norman strongholds guarding the crossings over rivers in the coastal area. It was built at a point reached by the high tide at the head of the estuary so that communication was still possible after a Welsh attack from the mountains had surrounded the castle and cut the roads.

Henry I granted the district to Roger, Bishop of Salisbury in 1106 and it was he who built the castle at the mouth of the river Gwendraethfach which was completed about 1115. Records show that the castle was in the hands of the Welsh in 1190, recaptured by the Normans before 1201, held again by the Welsh from 1215 to 1220 and from 1233 until about 1244. On the Norman side it passed through the hands of descendants of William de Londres and became part of the possessions of the Crown on the accession of Henry IV.

Today's visitor can see the original semi-circular moat and the 13th century curtain wall and towers of the inner ward which is square with the chapel tower which projects towards the river. The outer curtain and strong gatehouse keep were built early in the 14th century. As the outer curtain walls were higher than the original curtain the towers of the inner ward had to be increased in height by another storey to command the outer defences.

Approaching the castle the visitor will see the main gateway through the old town walls.

Manorbier Castle

Manorbier shows all the features of a medieval community with the castle, church, mill, dovecote and fishpond all around the seat of the feudal lord. It was originally a Norman earthwork and wood castle and the earliest lord recorded is Odo de Barri who died in 1130. The overlord was the steward of Pembroke Castle.

After the Norman invasion of the south west of Wales colonies of Flemings were established in Pembrokeshire and they were probably the workmen who built the stone castle for William de Barri to replace the original. His son Gerald was later known as Giraldus Cambrensis, a historian of the period – most sons became professional soldiers. Giraldus describes the garrison being called to arms in 1153 to repel attacks by the Welsh. In praising his family home he says that Manorbier, 'by its vicinity to Ireland is tempered by salubrious air'.

Few alterations have been made to the castle since it was built by the de Barris in the 12th and 13th centuries. In the Inner Ward the square tower at the gate still remains from the 12th century as do the round tower at the east corner and the baronial tower. Apparently the castle never had a keep but was an enclosure of towers linked by high curtain walls with a strong gatehouse with a portcullis archway. A watergate was one of the additions made in the 14th century.

Llanstephan Castle

This castle had a very confused history which in Norman times illustrated the precarious hold on the area of Carmarthenshire. What was a simple earth and timber castle originally was strengthened, increased and altered by successive occupants while repeatedly changing hands.

It was first recorded as captured by the Welsh in 1146 and they held it against English counter attack. It was captured and recaptured by the Welsh and the English from then until it came into the hands of Owen Glendower in 1405–6 during his rebellion. It also changed hands many times when in the possession of the English sometimes because the direct line of succession died out, sometimes passing into the hands of the Crown and subsequently being granted to different individuals. It finally became Crown property after the death of Jasper Tudor in 1495.

The castle consists of an upper ward above the steepest slope and a lower ward, protected by ditches cut in the rock. The upper ward is the older part of the building to which had been added a square tower at the inner gate.

It is the great gatehouse which is the most striking feature. This was the gatehouse to the outer ward, later converted into a strong keep by filling in the entrance. Above the original entrance is a chute for dropping water – no doubt intended to foil any attempt to burn the gate.

88

Narberth Castle

Narberth stands between Pembroke and the Prescelli mountains near the eastern border of Pembrokeshire. Southern Pembrokeshire was invaded more quickly and held more continuously by the Normans than other areas and settled more quickly especially with the help of Flemish immigrants who were soon absorbed into the English colony.

Pembroke castle provided the strength of the area and when other districts in the north were conquered, castles were built at Cardigan and Cilgerran, Nevern, Emlyn, and Narberth.

Of Narberth little now remains, and there is no trace of the original Norman castle of earthworks, mound and bailey. Still standing are some of the drum towers of a later stone castle built by Sir Andrew Perrot in the reign of Henry III. He was the grandson of the original builder, Stephen Perrot. This original castle was destroyed by Gruffydd ap Rhys just as the later one was taken and damaged by Llywelyn ap Gruffydd in 1256. However it was restored and was inhabited up to 1657.

Newport Castle

The castle dates from 1171. It survived into the period of the Wars of the Roses, was remodelled in 1448 and was finally battered into ruins by Cromwell's troops.

To the visitor the most interesting feature of the castle is the central tower with the hall or chapel above and the watergate below giving access from the River Usk.

This is one of the best preserved watergates in Britain. The watergate projects into the river, which is tidal at this point so that, when the tide was in, there was a pool of water in the lower storey of the tower by which boats could enter and unload at the quay at the far end. The entrance was protected by a portcullis, a narrow machicolation and a very strong double door.

It is only the east front of the rectangular bailey that survives. On either end is a tower. Inside, the two towers are square but they are octagonal on the outside, with tall spurs rising from the corners of the square bases. The visitor has a good view of these details from the bridge when the tide is out.

Ogmore Castle

Ogmore stands close to the Bristol Channel where the village of Ogmore-by-Sea is now two miles from the castle, which is in a romantic setting on the River Ewenny. Its position guards the ford which still has the stepping stones which attract many visitors to the spot.

Cardiff was the headquarters of the Norman penetration of Glamorgan, which was then the principality of Morgannwg, under Robert FitzHamon. His followers built the first mound and bailey castles at Coity Ogmore and other sites in the area. William de Londres was probably responsible for the oval inner ward surrounded by a deep ditch. It is interesting to see a part of the original earthworks on the south side of the inner ward.

Maurice, his son, probably built the rectangular stone keep. On the first floor of the west wall is a stone fireplace with a hood that gives the visitor some indication of the domestic life of the Norman conquerors. The outer ward of the castle was probably built in the 13th century.

A stone used in the medieval castle apparently came from an earlier church evidently dating from the 10th century as the inscription on it reads – 'be it known to all that Arthmail has given this field to God, to St. Glywys and St. Nertat and to Fili the bishop'.

Pembroke Castle

When Arnulph de Montgomery came to Pembroke in 1093 in the reign of William II he built a castle by digging a ditch from one side of the headland to the other and fortified it with a palissade and turf. It was in a strong defensive position at the end of a rocky ridge with steep sides and Pembroke river and marshes surrounding the ridge.

It was no coincidence that Arnulph de Montgomery arrived by sea; it proved difficult for the Normans to control the hills and mountains in South Wales and Pembroke became important as a stronghold and later as a base for their operations in Ireland.

The later custodian of the castle, Gerald de Windsor, married a Welsh princess, Nesta, and the power of Pembroke was increased further when Gilbert de Clare, called Strongbow, was created Earl of Pembroke in 1138. As one of the Lord Marchers of Wales he acted virtually as Regent in his own domain, and as succeeding Earls of Pembroke increased in power so additions were made to the castle. By the end of the 13th century, with greater prosperity, there was a need to protect the townsmen and a strong town wall was built.

During the Civil War Pembroke was at first the one major foothold for Parliament in South Wales and was only saved from the Royalist forces in 1644 by the arrival of a fleet in Milford Haven. Cromwell ordered the destruction of the castle by gunpowder but fortunately for the visitor today, it was too difficult to carry out this order properly.

Raglan Castle

Raglan is one of the finest castles in the whole of the Marches and the most beautiful and extensive castle in the old Welsh border district of Gwent. It still displays its machicolated towers in clean dressed stone of the 15th century and a great tower surrounded by a moat, which is still filled today, and reached only by a first storey bridge.

The great tower is a magnificent example of a self-contained fortified dwelling. In the 15th century it was necessary for the lord of the castle to have a safe retreat for himself and his family in the event of any attack by his own followers.

The gatehouse replaced the original main entrance through the south gate; it is very strongly defended by drawbridge, doors and two portcullises.

The castle is a stately monument to the Herbert family and was the judicial and administrative centre of the region. The present buildings, ranged around two courts and divided by a moat from the great tower are chiefly the work of Sir William Herbert. The heart of Royalist organisation in the west during the Civil War, Raglan capitulated only after Sir Thomas Fairfax surrounded it with three thousand five hundred troops. The castle, which was slighted by the Parliamentarians, is a stone's throw from the modern dual carriageway A40 road landscaped between the wooded slopes and the valley of the river.

Rhuddlan Castle

Rhuddlan stands at what was the lowest fording-place for crossing the river Clwyd and the coastal marshes.

The Normans threw up a defence round there and the Domesday Book of 1085 records a small borough with sufficient commerce to have its own mint where silver coins were minted from the reign of William I to that of Henry III.

The weakness of the English throne under Henry III allowed Llewelyn ap Gruffydd to establish himself and Edward I, after his return to England from the Crusade, found it necessary in 1276 to prepare for a campaign in Wales, concentrating men and material at Chester. The campaign of 1277 was soon over; advanced headquarters were established first at Flint and later at Rhuddlan with ships in support. Rhuddlan Castle was built for Edward I under the direction of James of St. George with round towers, gatehouses and thick curtain walls. Up to eighteen hundred men were employed. Work was interrupted by the second campaign against the Welsh when the castle was nearly finished in 1282–3. A new borough with defences to the north was established at the opposite end to the Norman borough which had centred around the old Norman mound and bailey castle.

The importance of access from the sea was underlined by the River Clwyd being diverted into a straight deep water canal up to the castle.

From Rhuddlan Edward I issued the Statute of Wales in 1284 that established the judicial control of most of Wales until the Act of Union in 1536.

Index to Illustrations